Walt Disney's
DONALD DUCK
ADVENTURES

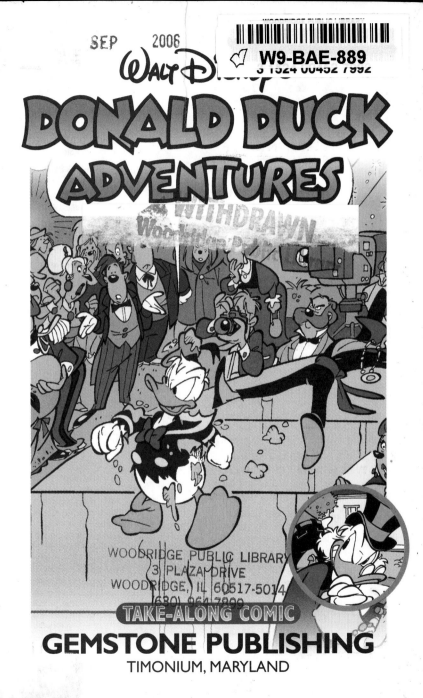

TAKE-ALONG COMIC

GEMSTONE PUBLISHING
TIMONIUM, MARYLAND

STEPHEN A. GEPPI
*President/Publisher and
Chief Executive Officer*

JOHN K. SNYDER JR.
Chief Administrative Officer

STAFF

LEONARD (JOHN) CLARK
Editor-in-Chief

GARY LEACH
Art Director

SUSAN DAIGLE-LEACH
Production Manager

MELISSA BOWERSOX
Director-Creative Projects

• IN THIS ISSUE •

Uncle Scrooge
ANOTHER DAY, ANOTHER DOLOR
Story: Spectrum Associates **Art:** Fecchi
Dialogue: Annette Roman **Lettering:** Gary Leach

Mickey Mouse
THE ROAD TO HOOLA-HOOPA
Story: Paul Halas **Art:** J. Gonzalez
Dialogue: Rick Thomas **Lettering:** Gary Leach

Donald Duck
BLUE RAIN
Story: Lars Jensen **Art:** Flemming Anderson
Dialogue: Lars Jensen and David Gerstein
Lettering: David Gerstein

Original cover color and color for above stories
provided by **Egmont**
Color modifications by **Gary Leach**

Uncle Scrooge
SEAFOOD BLUES
Story: John Lustig **Art:** William Van Horn
Color: William Van Horn and Susan Daigle-Leach

**ADVERTISING/
MARKETING**

J.C. VAUGHN
Executive Editor
Toll Free
(888) 375-9800 Ext. 413
ads@gemstonepub.com

ARNOLD T. BLUMBERG
Editor

BRENDA BUSICK
Creative Director

JAMIE DAVID
Executive Liaison

SARA ORTT
Assistant Executive Liaison

MARK HUESMAN
Production Assistant

MIKE WILBUR
Shipping Manager

**WALT DISNEY'S
DONALD DUCK
ADVENTURES 4**
Take-Along Comic
January, 2004

Published by
Gemstone Publishing

© 2004 Disney Enterprises, Inc.,
except where noted.
All rights reserved.

PRINTED IN CANADA

EUREKA! I'VE *GOT* IT!

WHATEVER IT IS, IT SOUNDS SERIOUS! JUST HOPE IT ISN'T CATCHING!

SHOULD WE CALL A DOCTOR?

OR THE GUYS IN THE WHITE COATS WITH THE NETS?

HA! THERE'S NOTHING TO IT! I'VE BOILED DOWN A *LIBRARY* OF BUSINESS ADVICE INTO *TWO* SIMPLE PRINCIPLES!

YOU HAVE? WHAT ARE THEY?

I'LL SAVE YOU THE TROUBLE OF READING IT! PRINCIPLE 1: FIRST AND FOREMOST, MONEY *MAKES* MONEY! AND THE MAGIC INITIAL INVESTMENT IS A MEASLY $1000 BUCKS! AFTER THAT, MONEY MAKES ITSELF!

IF YOU NEED AN EGG TO GET A CHICKEN...

...AND A CHICKEN TO LAY AN EGG...

...THE POINT WE'RE TRYING TO MAKE IS...

I'M NOT TAKING UP CHICKEN FARMING!

OR ENTERING AN EGG-TOSS CONTEST! I'M TALKING DOLLARS AND SENSE!

PRINCIPLE 2: THE BUSINESS PLAN!

ALARMINGLY SOON, AT THE BIN...

HIYA, UNCLE! I NEED A TEENSY-WEENSY FAVOR!

FORGET IT! I'M NOT IN THE MOOD! MY SWIMMING FACILITIES ARE FILTHY! I HATE DOING THE BACKSTROKE IN DIRTY MONEY, BUT THE POOL BOY WANTS $10,000 TO CLEAN IT!

SO YOU NEED TO *LAUNDER* YOUR *MONEY?*

IN A MANNER OF SPEAKING! WORSE THAN THAT, MY GROSS AND NET MARGINS DON'T ADD UP AND I'M A *MILLION* SHY OF THIS MONTH'S GOAL-A ROUND TRILLION!

I'VE SQUEEZED MY BUSINESSES, INVESTMENTS, STOCKS, SHARES, HIGH-INTEREST DEPOSITS, AND LEMONS! I EVEN CHARGED A WAITER FOR THE PRIVILEGE OF DRESSING MY SALAD! BUT THE TOTAL STILL FALLS SHORT.

WHAT I NEED IS A *FRESH* INVESTMENT OPPORTUNITY! SOMETHING NEW, AS YET UNTRIED!

THEN THIS IS YOUR LUCKY DAY! THE ANSWER TO ALL YOUR WOES IS AT HAND!

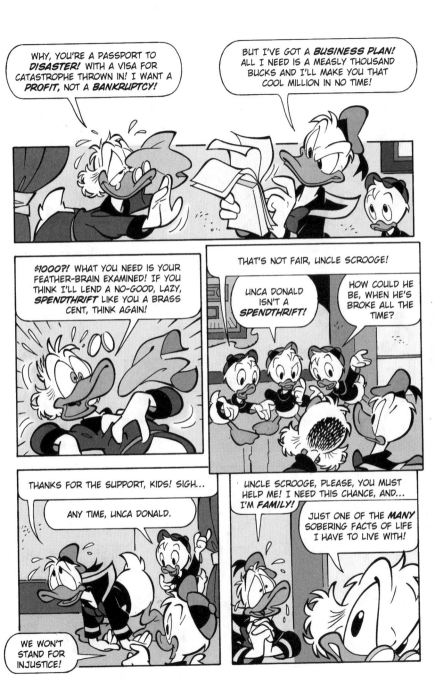

BUT THIS IS THE *OPPORTUNITY OF A LIFETIME!*

BAH!! OPPORTUNITIES TO THROW MONEY DOWN THE DRAIN ARE AS COMMON AS DIRT!

JUST TO SHOW I'M A *REASONABLE* MISER, THOUGH, I'LL RUN YOUR PROPOSAL THROUGH MY "AUTOMATIC IDIOTIC INVESTMENT ASSESSOR!"

TAP! TAP!

MAYBE I WAS A MITE HASTY! IT'S HAVING A NERVOUS BREAKDOWN!

RATTLE!

SHUDDER!

PHUT!

HUMMM!

SURPRISE, SURPRISE! ACCORDING TO THIS READOUT, ANY BUSINESS OF YOURS HAS AS MUCH CHANCE OF SUCCESS AS...CRYSTAL CHANDELIER JUGGLING...A CHINA SHOP STAFFED BY BULLS...BEAR-CAVE HONEY FARMING...AND UNDERWATER MINI-GOLF!

CALL ME IMPULSIVE, BUT SINCE YOU'RE FAMILY, I'LL LET YOU *EARN* YOUR SEED MONEY BY POLISHING MY CASH!

BUT THAT'S ONLY ONE-FIFTH OF...ONE-EIGHTH OF...*A LOT LESS* THAN THE POOL BOY CHARGES!

SLAP

TRUE, BUT YOU'RE AN AMATEUR! AND FACE IT, NEPHEW, YOU MAY BE ONE IN A MILLION, BUT THE ODDS OF YOU MAKING ONE ARE *A MILLION TO ONE!*

WHY, YOU MONEY-GRUBBING, TIGHT-FISTED, STINGY, OLD SKINFLINT! I DIDN'T COME HERE TO BE *INSULTED!*

NO? WHERE DO YOU *NORMALLY* GO?

HAW! I'VE ALWAYS *WANTED* TO USE THAT LINE!

COME ON, KIDS! THE OLD COOT HAD HIS CHANCE!

THUMP THUMP

HE'LL COME BEGGING AT THE FRONT DOOR OF OUR MANSION WHEN WE'RE LIVING IN THE LAP OF LUXURY!

MORE LIKELY WE'LL BE BEGGING...

...AT THE "ENTRANCE" OF OUR CARDBOARD BOX!

BACK AT THE HENHOUSE...

I DON'T MIND UNCA DONALD SELLING THE WASHER AND OUR BEDS, BUT...

...THE *TV?* OH, THE HUMANITY!

NOW HE'S ROUNDING UP ALL THE *"GREAT DEALS"* IN THE ATTIC HE PICKED UP AT YARD SALES LAST YEAR!

BANG

THUMP

DON'T TRY TO GRAB OUR JUNIOR WOODCHUCK GUIDEBOOK, UNCA DONALD! IT'S SALE, NEW OR USED, IS STRICTLY PROHIBITED!

OKAY, BUT I'M TAKING THE BOOKMARK!

THERE! THAT'LL ADD A FEW PENNIES!

BUT, UNCA DONALD! IS IT WISE TO SELL EVERYTHING YOU - AND WE - OWN?

THUMP

NOPE! WHICH IS WHY I'M TAKING IT ALL TO THE *PAWN SHOP.* THAT WAY I CAN BUY IT ALL BACK AS SOON AS WE'RE FILTHY RICH!

COME ON, YE WEE ONES OF LITTLE FAITH! HELP ME LUG THIS ALL DOWNTOWN! THERE'S NO TIME TO LOSE!

WHAT A STRANGE VASE...WITH SUCH STRANGE MARKINGS ON ITS BOTTOM!

YOU'LL HAVE STRANGE MARKINGS ON *YOUR* BOTTOMS IF YOU DON'T GET MOVING! TIME WAITS FOR NO DUCK! AND THIS DUCK HAS A DATE...

"...WITH DESTINY!"

CHECK IT OUT! PRETTY POSH STUFF, HUH?

PAWN SHOP

HOW MUCH SWAG FOR THESE SWANKY ITEMS?

HMM...

I'LL COPY DOWN THAT WEIRD WRITING.

AND CONSULT OUR WOODCHUCK MANUAL ON 'EM, SOON'S WE GET THE CHANCE.

CALL ME SOFT, BUT I'LL GIVE YA $900 FOR THE LOT!

IS THAT ALL?

DON'T PUSH YOUR LUCK, PAL! TAKE IT OR LEAVE IT! AND YA GOT THREE MONTHS TO REDEEM IT!

EH...RIGHT!

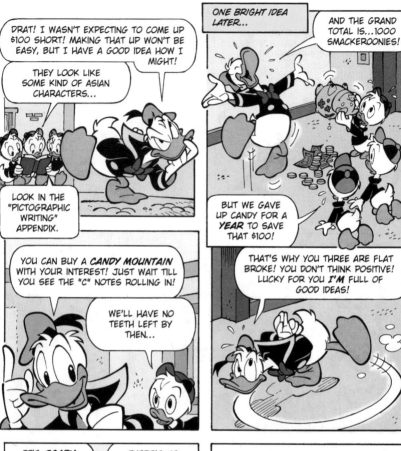

TIME TO CASH IN MY CHIPS!

HEY! WAIT UP!

BACK AT THE PAWN SHOP...

HI! I'M BACK TO REDEEM MY VALU...AH, I MEAN, *WORTHLESS* JUNK!

TRING

FINE! THAT'LL BE $100!

HUH? IT WAS ONLY WORTH $900 THIS MORNING!

INTEREST, STUPID! DON'T YOU KNOW NOTHIN' 'ABOUT BUSINESS?

INTEREST, SCHMINTEREST! I'LL BE RIGHT BACK WITH YOUR LITTLE "STORAGE FEE"!

WHERE'S THE VASE, UNCA DONALD?

STUCK IN HOCK TILL I FIND AN EXTRA DOLLAR SOMEWHERE!

INCREDIBLE! JUST *ONE DOLLAR* STANDS BETWEEN ME AND A *MILLION!* THE CHANCES OF THAT ARE A *MILLION TO ONE...*

"A MILLION TO ONE"... THERE'S AN IDEA...

I'VE GOT AN OFFER YOU CAN'T REFUSE! YOU'VE WOUNDED MY PRIDE AND NOW I'M THROWING DOWN THE GAUNTLET!

THIS OUGHTTA BE WORTH A FEW CHUCKLES!

GIMME ONE DOLLAR AND 24 HOURS, AND I'LL TURN IT INTO A MILLION!

YOU'LL *WHAT?!*

NEPHEW, YOU SHOULD BE A COMEDIAN, NOT A BUSINESSMAN! THE ONLY CENTS YOU GOT IS A SENSE OF *HUMOR!*

JUST LISTEN! IF I FAIL...

...I'LL POLISH EVERY COIN IN YOUR BIN UNTIL YOU CAN SEE YOUR UGLY MUG IN IT! FOR *FREE!*

YOU WILL?!

AGREED! HERE'S...HOLD IT! WHAT'S IN IT FOR *YOU?*

IF I *SUCCEED...*

...YOU GIVE ME *HALF* OF THE COINS I WAS GONNA POLISH!

WHOA! I DON'T LIKE THE SOUND OF THAT! I SENSE A *CATCH* IN THERE SOMEWHERE!

HA! SO IT'S TRUE WHAT THEY SAY! SCROOGE MCDUCK'S ALL TALK!

WHEN PUSH COMES TO SHOVE, HE FALLS DOWN! HE GETS COLD FEET! HE PADDLES FOR SHORE! WAIT TILL *THIS* GETS 'ROUND THE MILLIONAIRES CLUB!

BIG-SHOT MCDUCK TURNS DOWN A FREE BIN CLEANING 'CAUSE HE'S AFRAID HIS "NO-GOOD, LAZY, SPENDTHRIFT" NEPHEW COULD EARN THAT MILLION HE COULDN'T MAKE!

FINE! HERE! YOU ASKED FOR IT!

I TRIED TO BE NICE! TO PROTECT YOU FROM YOUR OWN FOOLHARDINESS! BUT YOU DON'T DESERVE IT! SO YOU'RE *ON!*

I CAN'T SAY YOU WON'T REGRET IT!

SURE YOU DON'T WANT TO BACK DOWN BEFORE IT'S TOO LATE?

SURE AS CAN BE! WHEN SCROOGE MCDUCK GIVES HIS WORD, IT'S AS RELIABLE AS A DICTIONARY FULL OF 'EM!

KISS THAT CASH GOODBYE, YOU OLD MISER! 'CAUSE, DULL OR SHINY, IT WON'T BE YOURS FOR LONG!

WE'LL SEE ABOUT THAT!

HOLD ON! THAT DOLLAR ISN'T A *GIFT!* IT'S A LOAN, AND THAT MEANS YOU HAVE TO SIGN FOR IT!

SLAP!

YOU'D CHISEL MOUNT EVEREST DOWN TO A KEYSTONE TO MAKE TEN CENTS!

ALL RIGHT, SMARTY-SPATS! WHAT'S THAT MEAN?

NO IDEA! IT'S A BAD-RISK CONTRACT DRAWN UP BY MY LEGAL EAGLES! LIKE IT OR LUMP IT!

AND DON'T THINK I'LL SKIP OVER READING THE SMALL PRINT! LESSEE, SAYS RIGHT HERE THAT...

"ALL LOANS SUBJECT TO INTEREST CALCULATED ACCORDING TO STANDARD HIGH-YIELD COMPOUNDING TERMS!"

I DON'T RECALL THE DETAILS! I'VE NEVER GOTTEN INTO THE HABIT OF MAKING HIGH-RISK LOANS! BUT SINCE YOU'RE SO CURIOUS...

...READ IT YOURSELF! IT'S ALL IN *HERE!*

THUMP!

SAVE IT! A BUSY BUSINESSMAN LIKE ME DOESN'T HAVE TIME FOR A CRASH COURSE IN LOAN SHARKING! THERE'S A MILLION WITH MY NAME ON AND I'M GOING AFTER IT!

DON'T LOOK SO DOWN, BOYS! YOUR UNCLE SCROOGE JUST GOT *SOMETHING* FOR *NOTHING!*

WE'VE GOT SOME BAD NEWS! BETTER SIT DOWN!

BETTER STILL, *LIE* DOWN!

ONE REVELATION LATER...

THAT NO-GOOD, DOUBLE-DEALING SCOUNDREL! HE HAD *INSIDE INFORMATION* AND NOW HE'S TRYING TO *PROFIT* FROM IT! HOW COULD HE DO THAT ME, HIS EVER-LOVIN' OL' UNCLE?

MAYBE 'CAUSE HE *LEARNED* IT FROM HIS EVER-LOVIN' OL' UNCA!

OH! WELL, NEVERMIND! THE POINT IS, HE'S MADE ME LOOK LIKE A *CHUMP!*

AND HE'S OUT TO GRAB UP *HALF* THE CONTENTS OF MY BIN! THAT'S NOT CHUMP CHANGE! I'VE GOT TO DO SOMETHING!

AND THAT MEANS TEACHING THAT DIRTY DEALER A LESSON HE WON'T SOON FORGET!

SIGH! ANOTHER ROUND OF INTER-DUCKAL WARFARE!

IT'LL ALL END IN TEARS!

WILL WHAT?

BEAT YOU!

YOU MEAN, YOU HAVE NO QUALMS ABOUT DOING THAT TO YOUR OLD UNCLE?

NOPE! IT'LL BE THE MOST FUN I'VE HAD IN YEARS!

YOU *MEAN* THAT?

SURE AS SHOOTIN'!

YOU'RE SAYING IT'LL BE *FUN* BEATING ME AND TAKING MY MONEY? IS *THAT* WHAT YOU'RE SAYING?

YES! WHAT'S THE MATTER, YOU'RE EARS PLUGGED UP OR SOMETHING?!

THE KA-CHING OF CASH REGISTERS HAS RUINED MY HEARING!

I SAID, I'M GONNA BEAT YOU AND TAKE YOUR MONEY!

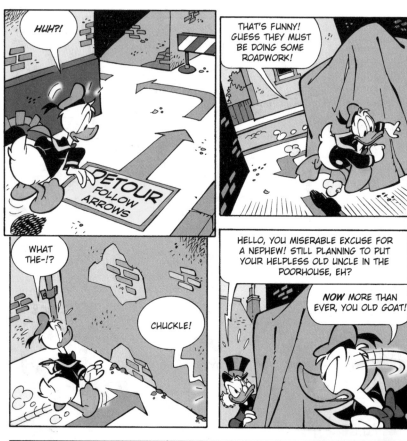

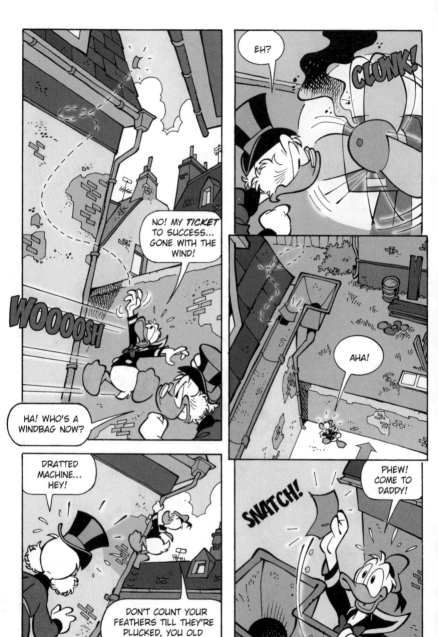

NEARBY...

AND NOW, LADIEEEES AND GENTLEMEEEN, I PREESENT MY FLAGSHIP VISION FOR ZE TRENDY, UP-AND-COMING YOUNG DUCKBURG EXECUTIVE!

DUCKBURG BUSINESS FASHION SHOW

YESSIR! THIS IS GONNA BRING DOWN THE HOUSE!

AIIIEE!

CRASH!

SACRE BLEU!

THUMP!

EEK!

GURF!

WHACK!

SHEESH! THIS IS GETTIN' TO BE A HABIT!

GAWSP!

PREPARE TO BE DAZZLED! LADIEEES AND GENTLEMEEEN, I GIVE YOU ZE CREME-DE-LA-CREME OF CORPORATE POWER SUITS - ZE *FLAME BIRD!*

YOU GOT *THAT* RIGHT, CHUM! PRESENTING ONE DONALD DUCK, ROASTED TO A TURN!

OH, MY!

GUESS I WASN'T THE SPECTACLE HE EXPECTED!

THUD!

SHORTLY...

YIPES! IT CAN'T BE!

PAWN SHOP

THAT NOODLEBRAIN NEPHEW OF MINE *PERSISTS* WITH HIS MISSION TO IMPOVERISH ME!

BUT HE'S IN FOR ANOTHER SURPRISE!

WE BETTER KEEP TABS ON UNCA SCROOGE!

PEELED BANANAS! WHAT'S THIS ABOUT? SOMETHING INVOLVING *MONKEYS*?

MAYBE, BUT WHERE'D ALL THE *SKINS* GO?

EITHER THIS IS THE WORK OF A CONFUSED CHIMP, OR UNCA SCROOGE IS UP TO SOMETHING MIGHTY SLIPPERY!

AT THAT MOMENT...

GREAT! NO SIGN OF THE OLD MISER! IT'S NOW OR...

...NEVER!

PHEW! MADE IT!

WOW! I'VE SEEN SOME FOLKS GO DOWNHILL PRETTY FAST AFTER THEY HOCK THEIR STUFF, BUT THIS IS A *RECORD!*

OKAY, SO I'M NO BOUQUET OF LILACS! JUST GIMME MY VASE, QUICK! I'M A MAN ON A MISSION!

THE REST YOU CAN SELL, TOSS, OR HANG ON A CHRISTMAS TREE! THIS LITTLE BABY IS ALL I NEED!

BAD ENOUGH TO HAVE MY HOPES AND DREAMS *SMASHED* LIKE THIS...BUT THAT MONEY-GRUBBING OLD MISER GETS THE LAST *LAUGH*, TOO...

HEAVENS! ARE YOU OKAY, PAL?

SIGH! APART FROM LOSING SEVERAL UMPTILLION DOLLARS, JUST DANDY!

BOY! THOSE TWO ARE A LONG WAY DOWN THE LADDER...I GUESS I SHOULD COUNT MY BLESSINGS!

SCREECH!

ZO! AT LAST I FIND ZE *CRETIN* WHO PREEMPTS MY SHOW AND THROWS EET INTO ZE CHAOS! EET EES *YOU!*

GULP! MAYBE I SPOKE TOO SOON!

IF YOU'RE LOOKING TO GET A PIECE OF ME, YOU'LL HAVE TO SWEEP IT OFF THE SIDEWALK...

OH ZO, MEESTER GATE-CRASHEER? WELL, ZIS EES ZE *PAYBACK* TIME...

WE'RE TALKING BUSINESS HERE, THE LAW OF THE CONCRETE JUNGLE, WHERE A *DEAL IS A DEAL!* WE WENT NOSE TO NOSE, AND THE BEST MAN WON! WHEN YOU GROW UP, YOU'LL UNDERSTAND! ISN'T THAT RIGHT, NEPHEW?

BAH!!

AND I'LL EVEN SEE YOU TO A GLASS OF MY VINTAGE CREME SODA! CALL ME EXTRAVAGANT, BUT THAT'S MY NATURE!

ENJOY YOUR EXTRA-VAGANCE WHILE YOU CAN!

CHEERS!

DON'T WORRY, UNCA DONALD! WE HEARD ABOUT WHAT HAPPENED!

AND WE'LL HELP POLISH ALL THOSE COINS!

'CAUSE I'M ABOUT TO TAKE THE SPARKLE OUT OF YOUR EYES AND THE SPRING OUT OF YOUR STEP! AND I'M GONNA ENJOY EVERY MOMENT!

ENTRE, HENRI!

BONJOUR, EVERYBODY!

ZE DONALD WANTS VOUS TO WITNESS MOI GIVING TO HEEM ZIS CHEQUE FOR UN *MILLION DOLLAIRS*! VOILA!

SPLUUUTTTT!

A M-MILLION DOLLARS! FOR *WHAT*?

ZE DONALD'S *PUNK OFFICE-CHIC* IDEA! EET HAS TAKEN ZE FASHION WORLD BY STORM, AND GEEVES NEW MEANING TO CASUAL FRIDAYS!

MERCI BEAUCOUP, HENRI! THE RIGHTS ARE YOURS!

ADIEU, UNCLE! LOOKS LIKE YOU'RE OUT ON ZE EAR!

IMPOSSIBLE!

EAT YOUR HEART OUT, YOU OLD SKINFLINT! LIKE YOU SAID, *A DEAL IS A DEAL!* AND I BEAT YOU LIKE AN OLD RUG!

BUT, BUT...

I NEVER JOKE ABOUT FIGURES! IT'S ALL HERE IN BLACK AND WHITE!

"INTEREST ON ALL LOANS CALCULATED AT 100% PER 3-MINUTE INTERVAL."

YES! AND YOU'VE HAD THAT LOAN FOR OVER 192 MINUTES! IF YOU DON'T PAY ME BACK QUICKLY YOU'LL OWE ME ALL MY MONEY AND A *GOOGLE* BESIDES! BWA-HA-HA...

100%... *EVERY THREE MINUTES!?*

BUT, HEY, I'M NOTHING IF NOT A REALIST! I'LL SETTLE FOR WHAT I CAN GET! THAT CHECK, FOR INSTANCE – JUST ENOUGH TO MAKE UP MY SHORTFALL THIS MONTH!

HMM...ACCORDING TO MY NOTES, THERE'S ONLY ONE DRAWBACK TO WEALTH...

AND AS SOON AS YOU FINISH POLISHING THE COINS MY MONEY BIN, WE'LL CALL IT EVEN!

REALLY? WHAT'S THAT?

SWIP!

YOU GOTTA HAVE YOUR HEALTH TO REALLY ENJOY IT!

SO? THERE'S NOTHING WRONG WITH MY HEALTH! I'M AS FIT AS A FIDDLE!

YEAH? WELL, PICTURE A FIDDLE RUN OVER BY A TRUCK! OR TRAMPLED BY A HERD OF ELEPHANTS! OR FED THROUGH A PASTA MACHINE...SLOWLY!

I'D NEVER CALL YOU THAT, GOOFY! IT'S JUST THAT SOMETIMES YOU CAN BE A LITTLE, UH, *GULLIBLE!*

WELL, WE'LL SEE JUST HOW GULLY-BULL I AM WHEN I'M A *SPAGHETTI MILLIONAIRE!*

YOU AREN'T GOING *THROUGH* WITH SUCH A CRAZY IDEA?

SO I'M *CRAZY* TOO?!

WELL, AS MISTER MOUSE HAS SUCH A LOW OPINION OF MUH BUSINESS SAVVY...

...MAYBE I'M BETTER OFF RUNNIN' TH' PLAN-TATION BY MUHSELF!

HE'LL COME TO HIS SENSES, I'M SURE...

THEN AGAIN, HE CAN GET KINDA STUBBORN SOME-TIMES, THE BIG DOPE!

TOCK!

LATER...

FOR SALE

GOOFY

HOLEY CHEESE! THE BIG GALOOT'S ACTUALLY HEADIN' FOR HOOLA-HOOPA!

MAYBE I CAN STILL CATCH HIM AT THE AIRPORT!

BUT...

YES, YOUR FRIEND LEFT FOR PORT KOWBONG, HOOLA-HOOPA, NOT TEN MINUTES AGO...

AIR MOUSTON

ACK! IF ONLY I'D RUN FASTER!

SMACK

HOLD ON! YOUR PAL TOOK THE ONLY DIRECT FLIGHT THIS WEEK, BUT I CAN ROUTE YOU THROUGH CONNECTIONS TO ARRIVE IN PORT COWBONG ONLY AN HOUR LATER!

HOT DOG!

BEFORE WHUT? ARE YOU *IN-CINERATIN'* I CAN'T LOOK AFTER MUHSELF?

NO, I JUST...

I GOT MUH TRIP TO THUH *INTERIOR* ALL ARRANGED! MUH GOOD FRIEND *AWANG* HERE HAS AGREED TO ACT AS SCOUT AN' PORTER!

YOUR GOOD FRIEND *WHERE?*

HUH? HE WUZ STANDIN' THERE JUST A MINUTE AGO, AN' NOW HE'S GONE...

...AN' SO'S ALL MUH *BAGGAGE!*

PLEASE GOOFY, GIVE UP THIS CRAZY QUEST BEFORE YOU END UP IN *REAL* TROUBLE!

WE CAN'T GO ON LIKE THIS, NOT SPEAKING TO EACH OTHER!

FRUMPH!

AFTER ALL, WE'RE *PALS* - THROUGH THICK AN' THIN, RAIN AN' SHINE...

HOKAY...

...THAT'S IF YUH DON'T MIND BEIN' PALS WITH SOMEONE WHOSE SO *GULLYBULL!*

TOGETHER MICKEY AND GOOFY WALK...AND WALK...AND WALK...

HMM...

UGH! PTOO!!

I DON'T KNOW WHAT THAT STUFF IS, BUT SPAGHETTI IT *AIN'T!*

WHUT A *SUCKER* I'VE BEEN! YET THAT FELLER HAD SUCH AN HONEST FACE...

HEY! I'M NOT SAYING YOU SHOULD BE SUSPICIOUS OF EVERYONE YOU MEET...

...BUT WHEN SOMEONE WANTS TO SELL YOU SOMETHING SIGHT UNSEEN, THAT'S A SURE SIGNAL TO BE ON YOUR GUARD!

IT'S JUST LIKE YUH SAID MICK, THAT FELLER SURE SAW ME COMIN'!

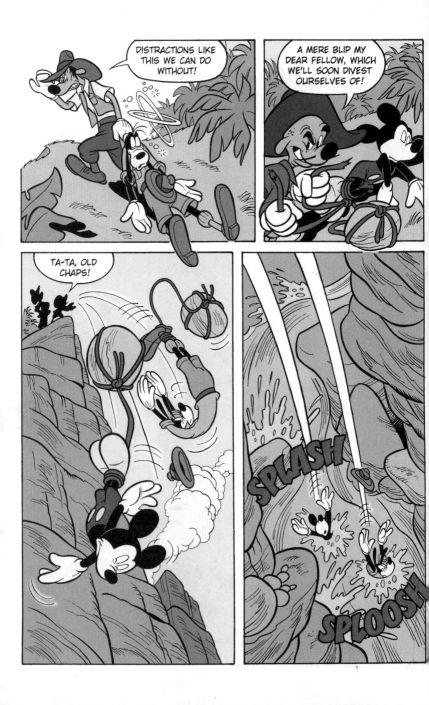

WE'RE JUST LUCKY THEY MISCALCULATED!

WHY DIDN'T THEM ROCKS SINK, MICK? BY RIGHTS WE OUGHTA BE *SUNK*!

THEY'RE PUMICE, LIGHT AND POROUS! I GUESS THIS AREA MUST BE *VOLCANIC*!

SO THEM GUYS WEREN'T BUTTERFLY HUNTERS AFTER ALL!

NOPE! GOTTA WONDER WHAT THEY *ARE* AFTER!

BEATS ME...ONE THING I DO KNOW, I'M *DOG TIRED*!

MAY AS WELL SLEEP HERE...YAWN!

IT MAY STINK O' SULPHUR, BUT TH' ROCK'S WARM!

ZZZ

MICKEY AND GOOFY ENJOY THE SLEEP OF THE JUST, UNTIL...

BZORK...

!?!

YOU GOTTA COME WIT US, UTTERWISE IT'LL BE *TOO BAD* FOR YOUSE!

'COURSE WE WILL, WON'T WE, MICK!

SAID TH' SPIDER TO TH' FLY! *LEG IT,* GOOFY!

BUT...

CLONK

GLUH!

LOOKS LIKE YOU WERE RIGHT TO TRUST THESE FOLKS!

SAW NO REASON NOT TO!

LOOK!

INCREDIBLE!

TH' SACRED *FIRE CREATURES!* THEY ONLY COME OUT FROM THEIR FIERY LAIRS ONCE OR TWICE A YEAR!

AND OUR TRIBE IS SWORN TO LET NO ONE DO 'EM ANY HARM! NO ONE!

PYGMY *TRICERATOPS!* FROM THE AGE OF THE *DINOSAURS!*

PURTY OLD, HUH?

MUST'VE ADAPTED SO WELL TO VOLCANIC ACTIVITY, THEY NOW *DEPEND* ON IT!

THEY GOT REAL LOVERLY COLORS - LIKE *BUTTERFLIES!*

HOLY SHMO! TH' "LEPIDOPTERISTS!" *NOW* I KNOW WHAT THOSE NETS AN' GRENADES WERE FOR!

WHOA!

CLACK!

OOOF!

HUP...THEY WON'T GET FAR NOW!

C'MON! I GOT TH' CREEPS WHO STOLE TH' *FIRE CREATURES!*

THIS IS TH' WAY WE HAUL IN THUH CHOPPER! YO HEAVE-HO, BOYS! HYUK!

OH, WHY DIDN'T I STICK TO BEING A *CHEAP SWINDLER*, LIKE NANNY SAID?

LISTEN, I'M GONNA CUT YOU A BREAK! BUT IF YOU EVER SHOW YOUR FACES 'ROUND HERE AGAIN, THAT *STEW POT* WILL BE WAITING!

YOU'VE SEEN THE LAST OF *US*, OLD FRUITS!

WE'RE GONE!

FORGOT TO MENTION YOU'RE *VEGANS*!

THE *YAM CURRY'S* READY! WHO WANTS CHUTNEY?

SAY, HERE'S THUH SPAGHETTI CREEPER!

YUM!

I GUESS IT ONLY NEEDED *COOKING!*

SLURP!

SO YOUR "SPAGHETTI" PLANTATION COULD TURN OUT TO BE A *GOLD MINE* AFTER ALL, GOOFY!

I DUNNO MICKEY...I DON'T THINK I'M CUT OUT FER LIFE IN TH' JUNGLE!

D'YA RECKON THUH MUSEUM WOULD TAKE ME ON? THIS WHOLE MISADVENTURE'S KINDA TAPPED ME OUT! I DON'T EVEN GOT A HOUSE!

NOT A CHANCE, PAL...I'M AFRAID I BURNT THAT BRIDGE TO A CINDER BEFORE COMIN' HERE!

HERE - I KNOWS YOU FOLK VALUE SUCH THINGS!

A-AN *EMERALD!*

WHATTAYA KNOW! THAT OUGHTA RECOVER TH' COSTS O' COMIN' OUT HERE FER BOTH OF US! HYUCK!

AND BUY BACK YOUR HOUSE!

HOW CAN WE THANK YOU?

THANK *YOU,* MY FRIENDS! ANYTIME YOU WANT A-ONE VEGAN CUISINE, JUST DROP BY!

THEY'RE SHURE *GOOD FOLKS!* GLAD T' KNOW 'EM!

YEP! AND YOU HAD 'EM PEGGED FROM THE START!

MORE DISNEY excitement TO COME!

If you like this comic, you'll want to be on board for all the fun in the months to come, with Gemstone Publishing's exciting line of Disney comic books.

For collectors: Walt Disney's Comics and Stories and Uncle Scrooge, providing the best of vintage and recent classic tales by such highly-acclaimed creators as Carl Barks, Pat Block, Daniel Branca, Cesar Ferioli, David Gerstein, Michael T. Gilbert, Daan Jippes, Don Markstein, Pat McGreal, Dave Rawson, Don Rosa, Noel Van Horn, William Van Horn, and many more. These books are 64 pages and in the sturdy, squarebound prestige format that collectors love.

For readers on the go: Donald Duck Adventures, the first title in our new 5" X 7½" "Take-Along Comic" series, gives you long adventure stories starring Mickey, Donald, Scrooge, and others in modern stories that take them beyond the limits of space and time.

©2003 Disney Enterprises, Inc.

For readers of all ages: Donald Duck and Mickey Mouse and Friends, offering Disney fans the best contemporary Mouse and Duck stories in the familiar 32-page, stapled, comic book format.

Look for them at your local comic shop! Can't find a comic shop? Try the Toll Free Comic Shop Locator Service at (888) COMIC BOOK for the shop nearest you! If you can't find Gemstone's Disney comics in your neighborhood you may subscribe at no extra charge, and we'll pay the postage! Use the coupon below, or a copy:

www.gemstonepub.com

Comic Characters
Delivered Weekly

When you log onto

SCOOP

Scoop is the FREE, weekly, e-newsletter from Gemstone Publishing and Diamond International Galleries for collectors and pop culture enthusiasts of all ages. It covers the past, present and future of comic character collectibles, the latest industry news, media happenings and so much more - to get you tuned into those trends that have shaped our history and our development as a society. Read the latest about the characters you love - and get to know other characters both old and new. So don't wait - visit **http://scoop.diamondgalleries.com** to check it all out!